JESUS LOVES YOU

Contact Us:

✉ MyBibleWorkbooks@gmail.com

📷 Projectkingdomcome

f Projectkingdomcome

PROJECT KINGDOM COME
ISBN 978-1-961786-09-7

Get The Entire Workbook Series!

SCAN ME

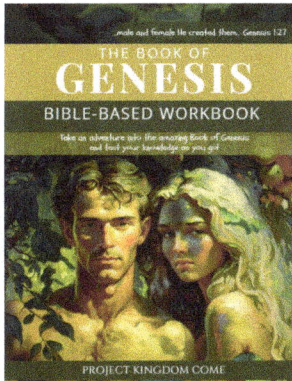
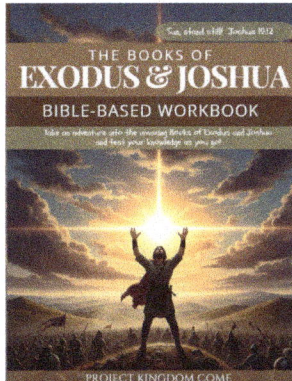
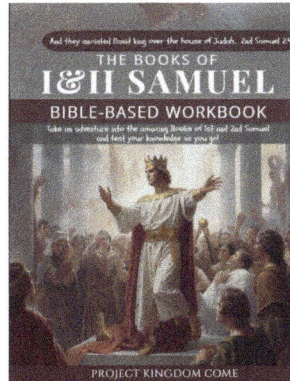

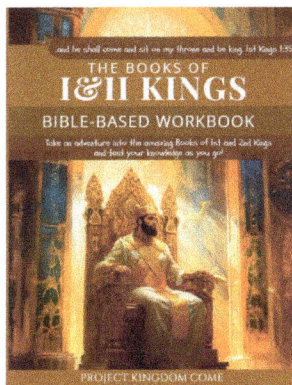
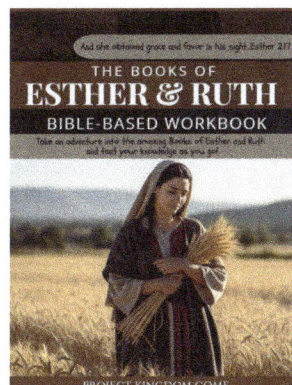
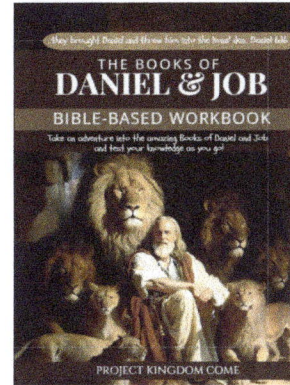

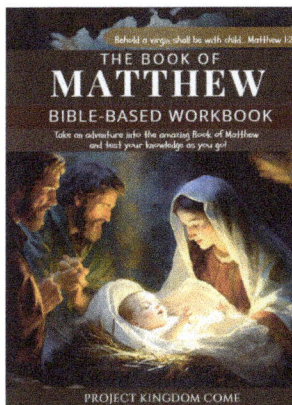
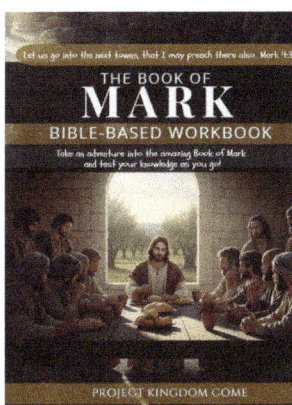
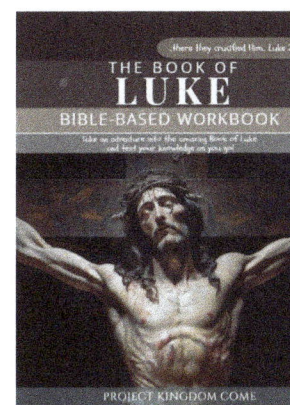

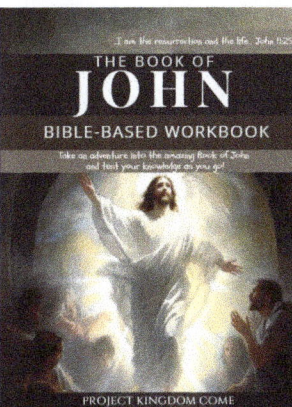
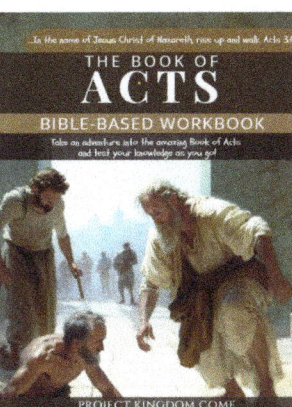
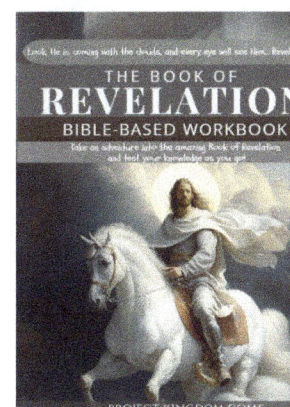

WWW.MYBIBLEWORKBOOKS.COM

This workbook belongs to:

_____

_____

_____

Leave your mark!

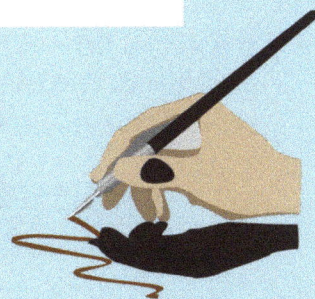

HOW TO USE THIS WORKBOOK

This workbook is designed to help young people explore the treasures in God's Word while having fun, growing in faith, and learning how to search the Scriptures for life's answers.

Here is what you will find inside:

Multiple Choice Questions
Each question comes directly from Scripture and includes a reference verse to help with locating the answer in the Bible. If possible, use a physical Bible to search for the answers.

Weekly Segments
Questions are grouped in weekly categories that could also be completed in a shorter or longer time frame.

Weekly Memory Verses
At the start of every week is a Bible verse to memorize. Each day of that week will repeat that memory verse with a chance to test memorization at the end of the week.

Certificate of Completion
At the end of the workbook, please find a Certificate of Achievement, ready for the child's name and parent or teacher's signature. Celebrate the accomplishment of studying an entire book in the Bible!

Answer Key
The workbook contains an answer key to serve as a support tool for parents or teachers reviewing the responses.

Recommendation for Parents and/or Teachers: Review the responses with your child or student and discuss lessons learned or interesting insights, to improve the child's retention and enrichment in the knowledge of God's word.

You can do all things through Christ who gives you strength!
Philippians 4:13

SAMPLE QUESTION...
HOW TO USE THIS WORKBOOK

Reading the reference verse will always lead you to the correct answer!

In the beginning was: (John 1:1)

(A) The Word
B. Heaven and Earth
C. Heaven only
D. Earth only

The number that comes after the book is the 'Chapter'

This is the name of a book in the Bible

John 1:1

The number after the chapter is the 'Verse'

NOW TEST YOURSELF! FIND JOSHUA CHAPTER 1 VERSE 8 IN YOUR BIBLE!

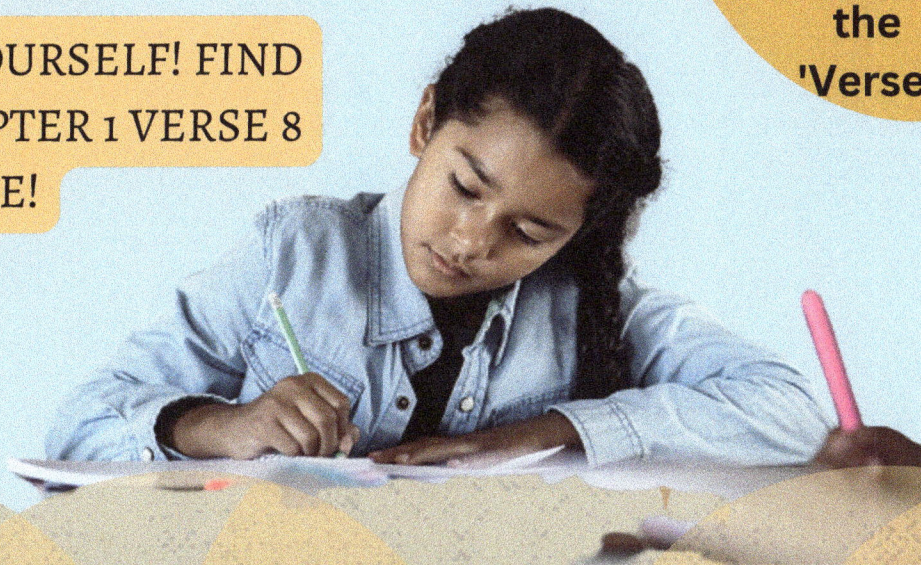

INTRODUCTION: THE BOOK OF JOHN

That You May Believe... and Have Life in His Name

The **Book of John** is a powerful Gospel written so that we may truly **know who Jesus is - the Son of God,** the **Word made flesh**, the **Savior of the world**. More than just a biography, John invites us into a personal encounter with Jesus, showing us **His miracles**, **His heart,** and **His glory**.

While the other Gospels focus on what Jesus did, **John focuses on who Jesus is**. Through rich storytelling and divine insight, John reveals Jesus as **the Bread of Life**, **the Good Shepherd**, **the Resurrection and the Life**, **the True Vine**, the **Light of the World**, and more...

As you journey through this book, you will see Jesus t**urning water into wine**, **healing the sick**, **washing His disciples' feet**, **raising the dead**, and ultimately **giving His life for us on the cross**. But John doesn't stop there—he also takes us into the empty tomb and the risen victory of Jesus!

As you go through this workbook, you will discover:
- **Who Jesus truly is through His "I AM" statements**
- **How belief in Jesus leads to eternal life**
- **The deep love and unity between Jesus and His Father**
- **The personal invitation Jesus gives to every heart**

So come with an open heart, ready to meet Jesus through every chapter & believe!

"But these are written that you may believe that Jesus is the Christ, the Son of God, and that believing you may have life in His name." - John 20:31

WEEK 1

1. Who was with God in the beginning? (John 1:1)

A. God's creation
B. The angels
C. The 24 elders
D. The Word

2. Who was also God, and through Him all things were made? (John 1:1-3)

A. God's creation
B. The angels
C. The 24 elders
D. The Word

3. Who was sent by God to testify about the Light so that all might believe through him? (John 1:6–7)

A. James
B. Jesus Christ
C. The Holy Spirit
D. John

WEEK 1 MEMORY VERSE: JOHN 1:1
In the beginning was the Word, and the Word was with God, and the Word was God.

4. What right is given to those who receive the true Light and believe in His name? (John 1:12)

A. The right to be the light
B. The right to be like the light
C. The right to become children of God
D. The right of free will

5. True or False: Those who receive the true Light are born again—not of blood, nor of the will of flesh, but of God. (John 1:12–13)

A. False
B. True

6. Who is the Word that became flesh and lived among us? (John 1:14–18)

A. God
B. Jesus Christ
C. The Holy Spirit
D. John

WEEK 1 MEMORY VERSE: JOHN 1:1
In the beginning was the Word, and the Word was with God, and the Word was God.

WEEK 1

7. What did John testify about the true Light? (John 1:15)

A. He would come after John
B. He was far greater than John
C. He existed before John did
D. All the above

8. Through whom did grace and truth come? (John 1:17)

A. John
B. Jesus Christ
C. The Holy Spirit
D. Peter

9. Who is the only one who has seen God and made Him known? (John 1:18)

A. John
B. The only begotten Son of God (Jesus Christ)
C. The Angel of the Lord
D. Peter

WEEK 1 MEMORY VERSE: JOHN 1:1
In the beginning was the Word, and the Word was with God, and the Word was God.

10. How did John respond when asked who he was? (John 1:19–23)

A. He said he was not the Christ
B. He said he was not Elijah
C. He said he was the voice of one crying in the wilderness
D. All the above

11. What was John's response when he was asked why he was baptizing? (John 1:24-27)

A. He did not respond
B. He said he had been given authority to baptize only with water
C. He confessed he should not be baptizing
D. He said he baptized with water, but someone greater was coming whose sandal strap he was unworthy to untie

12. At what location did John conduct baptisms? (John 1:28)

A. River Jordan
B. River Nile
C. The sea of Galilee
D. The Indian Ocean

WEEK 1 MEMORY VERSE: JOHN 1:1
In the beginning was the Word, and the Word was with God, and the Word was God.

13. When John said, "Behold, the Lamb of God who takes away the sin of the world" who was he referring to? (John 1:29-34)

A. God
B. Jesus Christ
C. The Holy Spirit
D. All the above

14. What sign confirmed to John that Jesus was the Son of God? (John 1:32–34)

A. John saw the Spirit come down like a dove and rest on Jesus
B. God told John that the Spirit would rest on the One who is His Son
C. He was not convinced
D. Both A and B

15. John baptized with water. What did Jesus baptized with? (John 1:33-34)

A. Oil
B. The Holy Spirit
C. Words
D. Prayers

WEEK 1 MEMORY VERSE: JOHN 1:1
In the beginning was the Word, and the Word was with God, and the Word was God.

WEEK 1

16. What does Rabbi mean? (John 1:37-38)

A. Teacher
B. God is with us
C. Messiah
D. Jesus

17. What does Messiah mean? (John 1:41)

A. Almighty
B. God is with us
C. The Christ
D. Teacher

18. What does Cephas mean? (John 1:42)

A. Teacher
B. Follower
C. Stone / Rock
D. The Christ

WEEK 1 MEMORY VERSE: JOHN 1:1
In the beginning was the Word, and the Word was with God, and the Word was God.

19. Whose name was changed to Cephas? (John 1:42)

A. John
B. Phillip
C. Mathew
D. Simon

20. Where did Jesus perform the first miracle? (John 2:11)

A. Capernaum
B. Canaan
C. Cana of Galilee
D. Jerusalem

21. What was the first miracle that Jesus performed? (John 2:1-11)

A. He healed a demon-possessed boy
B. He turned wine into water
C. He fed five thousand people with five loaves of bread and two fish
D. He turned water into wine at a wedding feast

WEEK 1 MEMORY VERSE: JOHN 1:1
In the beginning was the Word, and the Word was with God, and the Word was God.

> "The LORD keeps watch over me as I come and go, both now and forever (Psalms 121:7-8)"

Great job completing the week!

Did you memorize the daily verse?
Test yourself by writing it here...

_____

_____

_____

_____

_____

Use this space to draw a scene from the Bible or reflect on something you learned, felt or experienced...

WEEK 2

22. Why was Jesus upset when He went into the temple during Passover? (John 2:13–16)

AA. The people had turned the temple into a marketplace
 B. The Pharisees and Sadducees were making false accusations
 C. The temple leaders were teaching false doctrine
 D. The people were not celebrating Passover

23. What scripture was fulfilled when Jesus cleansed the temple? (John 2:17)

A. Love the Lord your God with all your heart
 B. Remember the Sabbath day and keep it holy
 C. You shall have no other gods before Me
 D. Zeal for Your house has eaten Me up

24. What did Jesus mean when He said, "Destroy this temple, and in three days I will raise it up"? (John 2:19–22)

A. He meant rebuilding the Temple in Jerusalem
B. He was referring to His body, which would resurrect after three days
C. He was a carpenter and could rebuild temples
D. He was threatening to destroy the temple

WEEK 2 MEMORY VERSE: JOHN 1:12
But as many as received Him, to them He gave the right to become children of God, to those who believe in His name.

25. Jesus knows what is in each person's heart. (John 2:23–25)

A. True
B. False

26. What made Nicodemus believe Jesus was sent by God? (John 3:1–2)

A. Because no one could perform such miracles unless God was with Him
B. He was a Pharisee and knew the law
C. He had a dream from God
D. He had the gift of discernment

27. What did Jesus say one MUST do in order to enter the kingdom of God? (John 3:3)

A. Show mercy
B. Love God with all their heart
C. Be born again
D. Do good to everyone

WEEK 2 MEMORY VERSE: JOHN 1:12
But as many as received Him, to them He gave the right to become children of God, to those who believe in His name.

WEEK 2

28. True or False: Being born again means being born of water and the Spirit. (John 3:4–5)

A. True

B. False

29. True or False: A person can physically return to their mother's womb to be born again? (John 3:4–5)

A. True

B. False

30. Complete this verse: As Moses lifted up the serpent in the wilderness…….. (John3:14)

A. The people were healed

B. The people were restored to their rightful place in Christ

C. God was able to perform signs, miracles, and wonders

D. The son of man must also be lifted up

WEEK 2 MEMORY VERSE: JOHN 1:12
But as many as received Him, to them He gave the right to become children of God, to those who believe in His name.

31. Why did Jesus say He must be lifted up? (John 3:14–15)

A. So that whoever believes in Him will not perish but have eternal life
B. So all may see Him as God
C. So people believe in His faithfulness
D. So people know He is powerful

32. What does John 3:16 say? (John 3:16)

A. God loved everyone and gave His Son so all who believe will live forever.
B. For God so loved the world that He gave His only begotten Son, that whoever believes in Him should not perish but have everlasting life.
C. God gave His Son so everyone who believes can enter God's kingdom.
D. God loved the world and gave His Son so people can believe and live forever.

33. Why did God send His Son into the world? (John 3:17)

A. To heal the sick
B. To perform miracles
C. That the world through Him might be saved
D. To cleanse lepers

WEEK 2 MEMORY VERSE: JOHN 1:12
But as many as received Him, to them He gave the right to become children of God, to those who believe in His name.

WEEK 2

34. Jesus did not come to the world to condemn the world but that through Him, the world may be saved (John 3:17)

A. True
B. False

35. Why are those that reject Christ condemned? (John 3:18-20)

A. They love the world (darkness) more than the Light (Christ)
B. They do evil and don't want their sin exposed
C. They choose to remain in darkness
D. All the above

36. Which of the following was NOT said by John about Jesus? (John 3:25–36)

A. I am not the Christ but sent before Him
B. He must increase, I must decrease
C. He who comes from above is above all
D. I have the honor to be His obedient servant

WEEK 2 MEMORY VERSE: JOHN 1:12
But as many as received Him, to them He gave the right to become children of God, to those who believe in His name.

WEEK 2

37. Those who believe in the Son have eternal life, but those who reject Him remain under judgment. (John 3:36)

A. True
B. False

38. What did Jesus ask of the Samaritan woman at the well? (John 4:7)

A. A place to stay
 B. Directions to the temple
C. Water to drink
 D. Supplies for the journey

39. Why was the Samaritan woman surprised that Jesus was talking to her? (John 4:9)

A. Because Jews didn't associate with Samaritans
B. Because she was a sinner
C. Because she was unmarried
D. Because she was divorced

WEEK 2 MEMORY VERSE: JOHN 1:12
But as many as received Him, to them He gave the right to become children of God, to those who believe in His name.

40. If the Samaritan woman had known who Jesus was, what would she have asked for? (John 4:10)

A. Healing
B. Power
C. Living water
D. Anointing

41. What happens to those who drink the water that Jesus gives? (John 4:13–14)

A. They will be refreshed
B. They will be filled
C. They will never thirst again
D. Their strength will be renewed

42. When the Samaritan woman asked where to worship, how did Jesus respond? (John 4:19–24)

A. Salvation is for the Jews who worship in Jerusalem
B. True worshipers will worship the Father in spirit and in truth
C. Samaritans should keep worshiping on the mountains
D. All the above

WEEK 2 MEMORY VERSE: JOHN 1:12
But as many as received Him, to them He gave the right to become children of God, to those who believe in His name.

> "My steps are ordered by the Lord, and He delights in every detail of my life (Psalm 37:23)

Great job completing the week!

Did you memorize the daily verse?
Test yourself by writing it here...

_____

_____

_____

_____

_____

_____

Use this space to draw a scene from the Bible or reflect
on something you learned, felt or experienced...

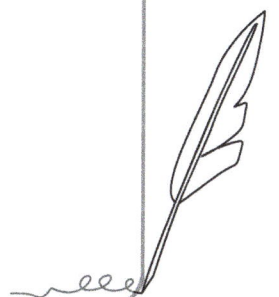

WEEK 3

43. True or False: God is Spirit, and those who worship Him must worship in spirit only. (John 4:24)

A. True
B. False

44. How did Jesus reveal Himself to the Samaritan woman? (John 4:25-26)

A. As the Son of David
B. As God
C. As the Messiah
D. He did not reveal Himself

45. What did Jesus say when the disciples urged Him to eat? (John 4:31-34)

A. He had another type of food to eat that they knew nothing about
B. His food was to do the will of the Father
C. Both A and B
D. He was fasting

WEEK 3 MEMORY VERSE: JOHN 3:16
For God so loved the world that He gave His only begotten Son, that whoever believes in Him should not perish but have everlasting life.

WEEK 3

46. What was the second miracle Jesus performed in Cana of Galilee? (John 4:46–54)

A. He healed a demon-possessed boy
B. He haled the nobleman's son who was near death
C. He fed five thousand people
D. He turned water into wine

47. Why were there sick people at the pool of Bethesda? (John 5:2–4)

A. They were waiting for an angel to stir the water
B. They were hoping to be healed by entering the water
C. They were waiting for the Messiah
D. Both A and B

48. What did Jesus say to the man who had been sick for 38 years? (John 5:5–9, 14)

A. "Do you want to be made well?"
B. "Take up your bed and walk."
C. "Sin no more, or something worse may happen."
D. All the above

WEEK 3 MEMORY VERSE: JOHN 3:16
For God so loved the world that He gave His only begotten Son, that whoever believes in Him should not perish but have everlasting life.

WEEK 3

49. How did the lame man respond when Jesus asked if he wanted to be healed? (John 5:5–7)

A. He had no one to help him
B. He couldn't get into the pool fast enough
C. Both A and B
D. He said "Yes"

50. Why did the Jews question the healed man at Bethesda? (John 5:9–10)

A. Because he was carrying his bed on the Sabbath
B. Because he was acting strange
C. Because he was singing and dancing
D. All the above

51. Why did the Jews want to kill Jesus after healing the man on the Sabbath? (John 5:18)

A. He made Himself equal with God by calling Him His Father
B. They disliked His teaching
C. They didn't believe He was the Christ
D. They were jealous of Him

WEEK 3 MEMORY VERSE: JOHN 3:16
For God so loved the world that He gave His only begotten Son, that whoever believes in Him should not perish but have everlasting life.

WEEK 3

52. The Father judges no one but has committed all judgment to the Son (John 5:22)

A. True
B. False

53. What is a requirement for having eternal life? (John 5:24)

A. Believing in Jesus, who was sent by God
B. Living a righteous life
C. Showing mercy
D. Giving to the poor

54. True or False: The dead will hear the voice of Jesus, and some will rise to eternal life while others will face judgment. (John 5:28–29)

A. True
B. False

WEEK 3 MEMORY VERSE: JOHN 3:16
For God so loved the world that He gave His only begotten Son, that whoever believes in Him should not perish but have everlasting life.

WEEK 3

55. Who was the human witness sent by God to testify about Jesus?
(John 5:31–33)

A. John
B. Moses
C. Isaiah
D. Jeremiah

56. Who did Jesus say would accuse the Jews to the Father?
(John 5:45–47)

A. John
B. Moses
C. Isaiah
D. Jeremiah

57. What food did the disciples have before Jesus fed 5000 men?
(John 6:9)

A. Two loaves and five fish
B. Two fish and five loaves of bread
C. Twelve baskets of fish
D. Twelve baskets of bread

WEEK 3 MEMORY VERSE: JOHN 3:16
For God so loved the world that He gave His only begotten Son, that
whoever believes in Him should not perish but have everlasting life.

WEEK 3

58. How much food remained after feeding the 5000?(John 6:10–13)

A. 12 baskets of fish
B. 12 baskets of bread
C. 12 baskets with leftover barley loaves
D. 7 baskets of fragments

59. What did Jesus tell the people to seek instead of perishable food? (John 6:27)

A. Eternal life, which the Son of Man gives
B. Preaching the Good News
C. Giving to the poor
D. Showing mercy to others

60. When asked how to do the works of God, what did Jesus say? (John 6:28–29)

A. Sell everything and follow Me
B. Give to the poor
C. Believe in the One God sent
D. All the above

WEEK 3 MEMORY VERSE: JOHN 3:16
For God so loved the world that He gave His only begotten Son, that whoever believes in Him should not perish but have everlasting life.

WEEK 3

61. Who is the bread of God? (John 6:33-35)

A. Jesus
B. The One who comes from heaven and gives life to the world
C. Both A and B
D. God the Father

62. No one can come to Jesus unless............... (John 6:44)

A. The Father draws them
B. They hear a sermon
C. Someone tells them the Gospel
D. All the above

63. Who has seen God?(John 6:46)

A. Only righteous people
B. The One who is from God (Jesus)
C. The faith heroes in the Old Testament
D. Abraham, Isaac, and Jacob

WEEK 3 MEMORY VERSE: JOHN 3:16

For God so loved the world that He gave His only begotten Son, that whoever believes in Him should not perish but have everlasting life.

> **My God supplies all my needs according to His glorious riches in Christ Jesus (Philippians 4:19)**

Great job completing the week!

**Did you memorize the daily verse?
Test yourself by writing it here...**

_____

_____

_____

_____

_____

**Use this space to draw a scene from the Bible or reflect
on something you learned, felt or experienced...**

WEEK 4

64. What happens to those who eat the flesh of the Son of Man and drink His blood? (John 6:53–58)

A. They will have eternal life (live forever)
B. Jesus will raise them up on the last day
C. They will remain in Jesus and He in them
D. All the above

65. The words of Jesus are spirit and life (John 6:63)

A. True
B. False

66. Which disciple did Jesus say would betray Him?(John 6:70–71)

A. Judas Iscariot
B. Thomas
C. Phillip
D. Judas, son of James

WEEK 4 MEMORY VERSE: JOHN 3:17
For God did not send His Son into the world to condemn the world, but that the world through Him might be saved.

WEEK 4

67. Jesus' brothers had faith in Him and believed in Him (John 7:1-5)

A. True
B. False

68. Why did Jesus' brothers urge Him to go to Judea?(John 7:1–5)

A. So His disciples could see His miracles
B. So the world would see His works
C. Because they didn't believe in Him
D. All the above

69. What did Jesus say is the reason the world hates Him? (John 7:7)

A. Because He exposes its evil deeds
B. Because they were jealous
C. Because they wanted to kill Him
D. Because the leaders were accusing Him

WEEK 4 MEMORY VERSE: JOHN 3:17
For God did not send His Son into the world to condemn the world, but that the world through Him might be saved.

WEEK 4

70. How should we judge others' actions? (John 7:21-24)

A. We should look beneath the surface and judge with righteous judgment
B. We should judge without being hypocritical
C. We should judge others as we would have them judge us
D. We should use our wisdom and judge fairly

71. What happens in the hearts of those who believe in Jesus? (John 7:37–39)

A. Their hearts will be full of joy
B. Their hearts will be merry
C. Their hearts will be cleansed
D. Out of their heart will flow rivers of living water

72. The authorities rejected Jesus because no prophet had ever come from Galilee (John 7:45-52)

A. True
B. False

WEEK 4 MEMORY VERSE: JOHN 3:17
For God did not send His Son into the world to condemn the world, but that the world through Him might be saved.

WEEK 4

73. According to the Law of Moses, what was the punishment for adultery? (John 8:5)

A. Stoning to death
B. Jail time
C. Banishment
D. Crucifixion

74. How did Jesus respond when asked what to do with the woman caught in adultery? (John 8:5-7)

A. He wrote on the ground
B. He said nothing at first
C. He told them the sinless one should throw the first stone
D. All the above

75. What did Jesus say to the woman caught in adultery after the accusers left? (John 8:10–11)

A. He prayed for her
B. He preached to her
C. He told her to go home and sin no more
D. He told her to ask for forgiveness from her husband

WEEK 4 MEMORY VERSE: JOHN 3:17
For God did not send His Son into the world to condemn the world, but that the world through Him might be saved.

WEEK 4

76. Who did Jesus say is the Light of the world?(John 8:12)

A. Moses
B. Jesus Christ
C. God
D. Holy Spirit

77. Who did Jesus say testifies about Him?(John 8:13–18)

A. God, the Father
B. The Law of Moses
C. The Holy Spirit
D. The angels

78. You shall know the truth.... How does this verse end? (John 8:32)

A. You will live forever
B. You will gain eternal life
C. The truth shall make you free
D. Jesus is the way, truth, and life

WEEK 4 MEMORY VERSE: JOHN 3:17
For God did not send His Son into the world to condemn the world, but that the world through Him might be saved.

WEEK 4

79. What happens if the Son sets you free?(John 8:36)

A. You will be free indeed
B. You will live forever
C. You will become God's child
D. You will set others free

80. Who is a liar and the father of lies? (John 8:44)

A. The world
B. The devil
C. All sinners
D. The Pharisees

81. Why did Jesus say, "you are of your father the devil"? (John 8:42-47)

A. Because they did not listen to God's words
B. Because they would love Jesus if God were their Father
C. Because they wanted to do evil like the devil
D. All the above

WEEK 4 MEMORY VERSE: JOHN 3:17
For God did not send His Son into the world to condemn the world, but that the world through Him might be saved.

WEEK 4

82. "Before Abraham was, I AM." Did Jesus say He existed before Abraham? (John 8:58)

A. True
B. False

83. Why was the man born blind?(John 9:1–3)

A. His parents sinned
B. He sinned
C. His family sinned
D. So that the works of God might be revealed in him

84. How did Jesus heal the man born blind?(John 9:6)

A. He rebuked a demon
B. He made mud with His saliva, spread it on the man's eyes, and told him to wash
C. He told him his faith made him well
D. He asked him if he believed

WEEK 4 MEMORY VERSE: JOHN 3:17
For God did not send His Son into the world to condemn the world, but that the world through Him might be saved.

"

As for me, I will call upon God; And the LORD shall save me (Psalm 55:16)

"

Great job completing the week!

Did you memorize the daily verse?
Test yourself by writing it here...

_____

_____

_____

_____

_____

_____

Use this space to draw a scene from the Bible or reflect
on something you learned, felt or experienced...

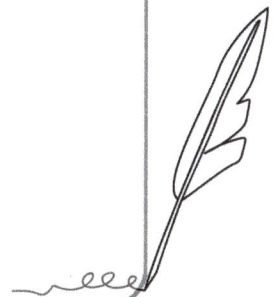

WEEK 5

85. Where did Jesus send the blind man to wash?(John 9:7)

A. River Jordan
B. The temple
C. The sea of Siloam
D. Pool of Siloam

86. What does Siloam mean? (John 9:7)

A. Sight
B. Sent
C. Seeing
D. Seek

87. What happened after the blind man was healed?(John 9:13–38)

A. He was questioned by the Pharisees
B. He was thrown out of the synagogue
C. He believed in Jesus and worshipped Him
D. All the above

WEEK 5 MEMORY VERSE: JOHN 10:10
The thief does not come except to steal, and to kill, and to destroy. I have come that they may have life, and that they may have it more abundantly.

WEEK 5

88. Jesus said He came to give sight to the blind and to show those who think they see that they are blind.(John 9:39)

A. True
B. False

89. What did Jesus say about the person who does not enter the sheep pen through the gate? (John 10:1–2)

A. He is the devil
B. He is a bad shepherd
C. He is a stranger
D. He is a thief and a robber, but the one who enters through the gate is the shepherd

90. A good shepherd knows his sheep and leads them.(John 10:3)

A. True
B. False

WEEK 5 MEMORY VERSE: JOHN 10:10
The thief does not come except to steal, and to kill, and to destroy. I have come that they may have life, and that they may have it more abundantly.

WEEK 5

91. What do the sheep do when they hear a stranger's voice? (John 10:4–5)

A. They run away and won't follow a stranger
B. They follow anyone who calls
C. They hide
D. They remain silent

92. Who is the door of the sheep? (John 10:7)

A. Jesus
B. The Holy Spirit
C. God the Father
D. The Shepherd

93. What is the thief's mission?

A. To steal, kill, and destroy
B. To steal only
C. To trick and confuse
D. To hide in the dark

WEEK 5 MEMORY VERSE: JOHN 10:10
The thief does not come except to steal, and to kill, and to destroy. I have come that they may have life, and that they may have it more abundantly.

WEEK 5

94. Why did Jesus say He came?(John 10:10)

A. So we may live and not die
B. So we may receive eternal life
C. To free us from the law
D. So we may have life and have it more abundantly

95. Who is the good shepherd? (John 10:11)

A. Jesus Christ
B. The Holy Spirit
C. God the Father
D. Religious Leaders

96. What does a hired worker do when a wolf comes?(John 10:12)

A. He finds the shepherd
B. He defends the sheep
C. He runs away and leaves the sheep
D. He fights with the wolf

WEEK 5 MEMORY VERSE: JOHN 10:10
The thief does not come except to steal, and to kill, and to destroy. I have come that they may have life, and that they may have it more abundantly.

WEEK 5

97. Jesus will gather all His sheep, even those not from this fold. (John 10:14–16)

A. True
B. False

98. Why did some say Jesus could not have a demon?(John 10:19–21)

A. A demon cannot speak as Jesus did
B. A demon cannot open the eyes of a blind man
C. Both A and B
D. None of the above

99. Why didn't some Jews believe Jesus was the Son of God? (John 10:24–26)

A. They were not His sheep
B. They did not believe His works
C. Both A and B
D. They believed He was the Son of God

WEEK 5 MEMORY VERSE: JOHN 10:10
The thief does not come except to steal, and to kill, and to destroy. I have come that they may have life, and that they may have it more abundantly.

WEEK 5

100. What are the characteristics of Jesus' sheep? (John 10:27-30)

A. They hear His voice
B. They follow Him
C. They are safe in His hand
D. All the above

101. Jesus said, "I and My Father are one." Did He say all creation is one with the Father? (John 10:30)

A. False
B. True

102. Why did the Jews accuse Jesus of blasphemy? (John 10:36)

A. They thought He was from the devil
B. He performed miracles
C. He healed on the Sabbath
D. Because He said He was the Son of God

WEEK 5 MEMORY VERSE: JOHN 10:10
The thief does not come except to steal, and to kill, and to destroy. I have come that they may have life, and that they may have it more abundantly.

WEEK 5

103. What message did Mary and Martha send to Jesus about their brother? (John 11:3)

A. He was dying
B. He was dead
C. He was sick
D. He was lost

104. What did Jesus say was the reason for Lazarus' condition? (John 11:4)

A. For the glory of God
B. Because he sinned
C. Because of Jewish punishment
D. Because he didn't believe

105. How many days did Jesus wait before going to see Lazarus? (John 11:6–7)

A. Four
B. One
C. Two
D. Three

WEEK 5 MEMORY VERSE: JOHN 10:10
The thief does not come except to steal, and to kill, and to destroy. I have come that they may have life, and that they may have it more abundantly.

"

I have life, and I have it more abundantly! (John 10:10)

"

Great job completing the week!

Did you memorize the daily verse?
Test yourself by writing it here...

_____

_____

_____

_____

_____

_____

Use this space to draw a scene from the Bible or reflect on something you learned, felt or experienced...

WEEK 6

106. Why did Jesus say He was going to see Lazarus?(John 11:11)

A. To find him
B. To wake him up
C. To pray for him
D. To cast out the demon

107. What did Jesus mean when he said Lazarus was sleeping? (John 11:11-14)

A. He was sick
B. He was dead
C. He was lazy
D. He was resting

108. Jesus is the _____ and the life.

A. Way
B. Truth
C. Resurrection
D. Roadway

WEEK 6 MEMORY VERSE: JOHN 11:25
Jesus said to her, 'I am the resurrection and the life. He who believes in Me, though he may die, he shall live.'

WEEK 6

109. What did Martha confess about Jesus?(John 11:27)

A. He is the Christ, the Son of God
B. He was a great teacher
C. He was a healer
D. He was the way and the truth

110. What is the shortest verse in the Bible, describing Jesus' response to Mary's grief? (John 11:35)

A. Jesus healed Lazarus
B. Jesus resurrected Lazarus
C. Jesus wept
D. Jesus was sad

111. What did Jesus do at Lazarus' tomb? (John 11:38–43)

A. Rolled away the stone
B. Prayed to the Father
C. Called Lazarus to come out
D. All the above

WEEK 6 MEMORY VERSE: JOHN 11:25
Jesus said to her, 'I am the resurrection and the life. He who believes in Me, though he may die, he shall live.'

WEEK 6

112. How long had Lazarus been dead? (John 11:39)

A. Four days
B. Two days
C. Three days
D. Ten days

113. What did the Pharisees and chief priests do after hearing of Lazarus' resurrection? (John 11:45–53)

A. They believed in Jesus
B. They brought the sick to Him
C. They plotted to kill Him
D. They joined His mission of preaching the gospel

114. Who was Caiaphas? (John 11:49)

A. A Pharisee
B. A High Priest
C. A Governor
D. An Emperor

WEEK 6 MEMORY VERSE: JOHN 11:25
Jesus said to her, 'I am the resurrection and the life. He who believes in Me, though he may die, he shall live.'

WEEK 6

115. What did Caiaphas unknowingly prophesy about concerning Jesus? (John 11:49–52)

A. Jesus would die for the nation
B. Jesus would gather the scattered children of God
C. Both A and B
D. He did not prophesy

116. Why did Mary anoint Jesus' feet with oil and wipe them with her hair? (John 12:3–7)

A. It was in preparation for His burial
B. She was thanking Him
C. She felt sorry for Him
D. None of the above

117. Which disciple said the oil could have been sold to help the poor? (John 12:4–5)

A. Peter
B. Caiaphas
C. John
D. Judas Iscariot

WEEK 6 MEMORY VERSE: JOHN 11:25
Jesus said to her, 'I am the resurrection and the life. He who believes in Me, though he may die, he shall live.'

WEEK 6

118. Why did the chief priests want to kill Lazarus?(John 12:9–11)

A. He was Jesus' friend
B. He was a tax collector
C. They wanted another miracle
D. Many people believed in Jesus because of Lazarus

119. What animal did Jesus ride during His triumphal entry? (John 12:14)

A. Horse
B. Donkey
C. Calf
D. Lion

120. True or False: Jesus said a grain of wheat must die in the ground to produce more grain. (John 12:24)

A. True
B. False

WEEK 6 MEMORY VERSE: JOHN 11:25
Jesus said to her, 'I am the resurrection and the life. He who believes in Me, though he may die, he shall live.'

WEEK 6

121. Jesus said that he who loves his life will _____ and he who hates his life in this world will _____ (John 12:25)

A. Lose it; keep it for eternity
B. Sustain it; lose it for eternity
C. Protect it; keep it for eternity
D. Lose it; lose it for eternity

122. What will the Father do to those who serve Jesus? (John 12:26)

A. Keep them
B. Honor them
C. Bless them
D. Sustain them

123. What happens when Jesus is lifted up? (John 12:32)

A. He draws all men to Himself
B. Nothing happens
C. The people live in peace
D. The people rejoice

WEEK 6 MEMORY VERSE: JOHN 11:25
Jesus said to her, 'I am the resurrection and the life. He who believes in Me, though he may die, he shall live.'

WEEK 6

124. Who is the Light of the world? (John 12:35-36 &46)

A. Jesus
B. The moon
C. The stars
D. The constellation

125. Why did some rulers believe in Jesus but not openly confess Him? (John 12:42–43)

A. They feared being kicked out of the synagogue
B. They loved praise from people more than praise from God
C. They did not believe Jesus was the Christ
D. Both A and B

126. Why did Jesus say He came into the world? (John 12:47)

A. To forgive the world
B. To save the world
C. To judge the world
D. To be the Light

WEEK 6 MEMORY VERSE: JOHN 11:25
Jesus said to her, 'I am the resurrection and the life. He who believes in Me, though he may die, he shall live.'

> "I increase in wisdom and stature, and in favor with God and men
> (Luke 2:52)"

Great job completing the week!

Did you memorize the daily verse?
Test yourself by writing it here...

_____

_____

_____

_____

_____

_____

Use this space to draw a scene from the Bible or reflect on something you learned, felt or experienced...

WEEK 7

127. Which disciple did not want Jesus to wash his feet at first? (John 13:6–8)

A. Simon Peter
B. John
C. Judas Iscariot
D. Matthew

128. What did Jesus say would happen if He didn't wash Peter's feet? (John 13:8)

A. He would not belong to Jesus
B. He would be disobedient
C. He would miss the blessing
D. He would have no part with Jesus

129. Why did Jesus wash His disciples' feet?(John 13:12–17)

A. He was teaching them that they should wash one another's feet
B. He was teaching them to do as He had done
C. They would be blessed if they did the things Jesus taught them to do
D. All the above

WEEK 7 MEMORY VERSE: JOHN 13:35
By this all will know that you are My disciples, if you have love for one another.

WEEK 7

130. How did Jesus identify the one who would betray him? (John 13:26)

A. He gave him a kiss
B. He gave him a piece of bread after dipping it
C. He shook his hand
D. He pointed at him

131. How will people know you are a follower of Jesus? (John 13:35)

A. By your love for one another
B. By washing each other's feet
C. By constant prayer
D. By attending church

132. What did Jesus say Peter would do before the rooster crowed? (John 13:38)

A. Deny Him three times
B. Betray Him
C. Follow Him
D. Die for Him

WEEK 7 MEMORY VERSE: JOHN 13:35
By this all will know that you are My disciples, if you have love for one another.

WEEK 7

133. Jesus said, "I am the way, the truth, and the life." (John 14:6)

A. True
B. False

134. Who is the only way to the Father?(John 14:6)

A. Jesus Christ
B. The Holy Spirit
C. Prayer and fasting
D. Earnest Prayer

135. If you have seen Jesus, you have seen the Father. (John 14:7–10)

A. True
B. False

WEEK 7 MEMORY VERSE: JOHN 13:35
By this all will know that you are My disciples, if you have love for one another.

WEEK 7

136. What will those who believe in Jesus do?(John 14:12)

A. Be saved
B. Be glorified
C. Do greater works than the works that Jesus did
D. Be blessed

137. In whose name should we ask anything of God? (John 14:13-14)

A. In Jesus' name
B. In the Holy Spirit's name
C. In the Father's name
D. In all three names

138. How do we show our love for Jesus? (John 14:15)

A. By keeping His commandments
B. By praying
C. By showing kindness
D. By worshiping

WEEK 7 MEMORY VERSE: JOHN 13:35
By this all will know that you are My disciples, if you have love for one another.

WEEK 7

139. Who is the Helper that Jesus promised to send?(John 14:16–17)

A. The Spirit of truth
B. The Holy Spirit
C. Both A and B
D. None of the above

140. To whom will Jesus reveal Himself? (John 14:21)

A. To those who love Him and obey His commands
B. To everyone
C. To all the saved
D. To the disciples only

141. What did Jesus say the Holy Spirit would do?(John 14:26)

A. Be our helper
B. Teach us all things
C. Remind us of everything Jesus said
D. All the above

WEEK 7 MEMORY VERSE: JOHN 13:35
By this all will know that you are My disciples, if you have love for one another.

WEEK 7

142. What did Jesus say He was giving to us? (John 14:27)

A. His peace
B. His joy
C. His love
D. His righteousness

143. Jesus said He is the true vine. Who is the vine dresser? (John 15:1)

A. The Helper
B. The Wine dresser
C. The Wine presser
D. God the Father

144. What does the Father do to the branch that bears fruit? (John 15:2)

A. He presses it
B. He prunes it
C. He discards it
D. He blesses it

WEEK 7 MEMORY VERSE: JOHN 13:35
By this all will know that you are My disciples, if you have love for one another.

WEEK 7

145. What happens to a branch that does not bear fruit? (John 15:2)

A. He presses it
B. He prunes it
C. He discards it
D. He blesses it

146. What must we do to bear fruit? (John 15:4)

A. Abide in Christ
B. Allow God to press us
C. Love one another
D. Keep God's commandments

147. If Jesus is the vine, who are we? (John 15:5)

A. The vineyard
B. The branches
C. The tree
D. The fruit

WEEK 7 MEMORY VERSE: JOHN 13:35
By this all will know that you are My disciples, if you have love for one another.

"

I will love others the
way Jesus loves me
(John 13:34)

"

Great job completing the week!

**Did you memorize the daily verse?
Test yourself by writing it here...**

_____

_____

_____

_____

_____

_____

**Use this space to draw a scene from the Bible or reflect
on something you learned, felt or experienced...**

WEEK 8

148. If we remain in Christ, and His words remain in us, we can ask anything and it will be done. (John 15:7)

A. True
B. False

149. True disciples bear much fruit to bring glory to God.(John 15:8)

A. True
B. False

150. Those who obey Jesus' commandments will remain in His _____. (John 15:10)

A. Heart
B. Mind
C. Love
D. Unity

WEEK 8 MEMORY VERSE: JOHN 14:6
Jesus said to him, 'I am the way, the truth, and the life. No one comes to the Father except through Me'

WEEK 8

151. There is no greater love than to _____ (John 15:13)

A. Love another
B. Love those who are unlovable
C. Show mercy to those that are unlovable
D. Lay down one's life for friends

152. Jesus said He no longer calls us servants but _____ (John 15:15)

A. Brothers
B. Brethren
C. Friends
D. Sons

153. Why does the world hate Jesus' followers? (John 15:18-19)

A. Because we are not of this world
B. Because it hated Jesus first
C. Because we have been chosen by Christ
D. All the above

WEEK 8 MEMORY VERSE: JOHN 14:6
Jesus said to him, 'I am the way, the truth, and the life. No one comes to the Father except through Me'

WEEK 8

154. If someone hates Jesus, do they also hate God the Father?
(John 15:23)

A. Yes

B. No

155. What did Jesus say is the benefit of Him going away?
(John 16:7–8)

A. He will send the Helper/Holy Spirit to us

B. He will send the Holy Spirit to convict the world of sin, righteousness, and judgment

C. Both A and B

D. Jesus did not say these words

156. What will the Spirit of Truth (Holy Spirit) do? (John 16:12–14)

A. Guide us into all truth

B. Show us things to come

C. Glorify Jesus

D. All the above

WEEK 8 MEMORY VERSE: JOHN 14:6

Jesus said to him, 'I am the way, the truth, and the life. No one comes to the Father except through Me'

WEEK 8

157. In whose name did Jesus say we should pray so the Father will answer us? (John 16:23–24)

A. The name of Jesus Christ
B. The name of the Holy Spirit
C. The name of God the Father
D. All the above

158. Where can we find true peace? (John 16:33)

A. Our family
B. Our neighbors
C. The Church
D. In Jesus Christ

159. What did Jesus say is eternal life? (John 17:3)

A. To know the one and only true God
B. To know Jesus Christ, who was sent of God
C. Obeying God's commandments
D. Both A and B

WEEK 8 MEMORY VERSE: JOHN 14:6
Jesus said to him, 'I am the way, the truth, and the life. No one comes to the Father except through Me'

WEEK 8

160. What did Jesus pray for concerning His disciples? (John 17:6-17)

A. That God would protect them
B. That God would keep them from the evil one
C. That God would sanctify them with the Word which is truth
D. All the above

161. What did Jesus ask of God concerning all that would ever believe in Him (John 17:20-26)

A. That they would be united as one
B. That they would be with Him and see His glory
C. That they would experience God's love
D. All the above

162. Who tried to defend Jesus by drawing a sword and cutting off a man's ear? (John 18:10)

A. John
B. Simon Peter
C. Mark
D. Luke

WEEK 8 MEMORY VERSE: JOHN 14:6
Jesus said to him, 'I am the way, the truth, and the life. No one comes to the Father except through Me'

WEEK 8

163. What part of the high priest's servant's body was cut off? (John 18:10)

A. Knee
B. Head
C. Neck
D. Ear

164. Jesus had predicted that Simon Peter would deny him _____ times before the _____ crowed? (John 18:17, 25-27)

A. Two times; the crow
B. Three times, the crow
C. Two times, the rooster
D. Three times, the rooster

165. What was the reason that Jesus came into the world? (John 18:37)

A. To bear witness to the truth
B. To condemn the world
C. To judge the world
D. All the above

WEEK 8 MEMORY VERSE: JOHN 14:6
Jesus said to him, 'I am the way, the truth, and the life. No one comes to the Father except through Me'

166. Who did the crowd ask Pilate to release instead of Jesus? (John 18:39–40)

A. Barabbas the murderer
B. Jesus Christ
C. Barabbas, the robber
D. Beelzebub

167. Which of the following is NOT something the soldiers did to mock Jesus? (John 19:2-3)

A. They twisted a crown of thorns and placed it on His head
B. They struck Him and mocked Him by saying, "Hail, King of the Jews!"
C. They put a purple robe on Him
D. They made Him carry a gold staff and sing a hymn

168. Why did the Jews say Jesus should die, according to their law? (John 19:7)

A. He preached in synagogues
B. He claimed to be the Son of God
C. He worked miracles
D. He disrespected Pilate

WEEK 8 MEMORY VERSE: JOHN 14:6
Jesus said to him, 'I am the way, the truth, and the life. No one comes to the Father except through Me'

" I love because He first loved me
(1 John 4:19) "

Great job completing the week!

Did you memorize the daily verse?
Test yourself by writing it here...

_____

_____

_____

_____

_____

_____

Use this space to draw a scene from the Bible or reflect
on something you learned, felt or experienced...

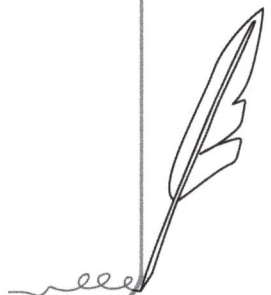

BONUS QUESTIONS

169. What is the meaning of Golgotha? (John 19:17)

A. Hell
B. A place of a skull
C. A place of gnashing of teeth
D. A place of sorrow

170. Who was present when Jesus was crucified and looking on from afar? (John 19:25-26)

A. Mary Magdalene
B. Mary, the mother of Jesus
C. John, the disciple Jesus loved
D. All the above

171. Who asked Pilate for Jesus' body?(John 19:38)

A. Joseph of Arimathea
B. Joseph of Galilee
C. Joseph the Nazarene
D. Joseph of Cupertino

MEMORY VERSE: JOHN 16:33
These things I have spoken to you, that in Me you may have peace. In the world you
will have tribulation; but be of good cheer, I have overcome the world.

BONUS QUESTIONS

172. Who brought myrrh and aloes to wrap Jesus' body?
(John 19:39–40)

A. Zacchaeus
B. Thomas
C. Nicodemus
D. Nebuchadnezzar

173. Who was NOT among the first to find Jesus' tomb empty?
(John 20:1–10)

A. Mary Magdalene
B. Luke
C. Matthew
D. Both B and C

174. Who was the first to see the risen Jesus and tell the others?
(John 20:11–18)

A. Mary Magdalene
B. Simon Peter
C. John
D. Matthew

MEMORY VERSE: JOHN 16:33
These things I have spoken to you, that in Me you may have peace. In the world you will have tribulation; but be of good cheer, I have overcome the world.

BONUS QUESTIONS

175. Which disciple did not believe Jesus had risen until he saw Him? (John 20:24–28)

A. Thomas
B. Simon Peter
C. John
D. Matthew

176. "Blessed are those who have not seen and yet have believed." Did Jesus say this? (John 20:29)

A. True
B. False

177. Why are the works of Jesus written in the Bible? (John 20:30-31)

A. That people may believe that Jesus is the Christ
B. That people may believe that Jesus is the Son of God
C. That people, by believing in Him, may have life by the power of His name
D. All the above

MEMORY VERSE: JOHN 16:33
These things I have spoken to you, that in Me you may have peace. In the world you will have tribulation; but be of good cheer, I have overcome the world.

BONUS QUESTIONS

178. Where did Jesus appear to His disciples the third time after rising from the dead? (John 21:1-14)

A. By the sea
B. At the corner house
C. On the rooftop of John's house
D. At the temple gate

179. Which instruction did Jesus NOT give Peter when He asked if Peter loved Him? (John 21:15–17)

A. Feed my lambs
B. Tend my sheep
C. Feed my sheep
D. Pray for my sheep

180. Who wrote the Book of John?(John 21:20–24)

A. Peter
B. The disciple whom Jesus loved (John)
C. Matthew
D. Luke

MEMORY VERSE: JOHN 16:33
These things I have spoken to you, that in Me you may have peace. In the world you will have tribulation; but be of good cheer, I have overcome the world.

"

I trust in God completely and have no fear. What can man do to me? (Psalm 56:11)

"

Great job completing the week!

Did you memorize the daily verse?
Test yourself by writing it here...

Use this space to draw a scene from the Bible or reflect on something you learned, felt or experienced...

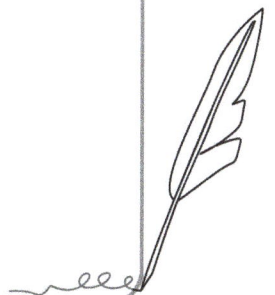

Certificate of Completion

This Certificate Certifies That:

_____

Has Successfully Completed The John Workbook!

Flo & Grace

_____   _____

PARENT/TEACHER SIGNATURE   **PROJECT KINGDOM COME**

WOULD YOU LIKE TO ACCEPT JESUS INTO YOUR HEART?

THE BIBLE SAYS:

If you confess with your mouth that Jesus is Lord and believe in your heart that God has raised Him from the dead, you will be saved **(Romans 10:9)**

SAY THE PRAYER BELOW OUT LOUD AND BELIEVE IT IN YOUR HEART!

Dear Lord Jesus,
I know that I am a sinner, and I ask for Your forgiveness.
I believe You died for my sins and rose from the dead.
I repent of my sins and invite You to come into my heart and life.
I want to trust and follow You as my Lord and Savior. Help me to live for you for the rest of my life.
I am now a child of God, and I ask You to fill me with Your Holy Spirit.

In Jesus' Name I pray, Amen.

Congratulations!
If you have prayed this prayer, please let an adult know or send an email to mybibleworkbooks@gmail.com

 **ANSWER KEY:**

1.D	13. B	25. A
2.D	14. D	26. A
3.D	15. B	27. C
4.C	16. A	28. A
5.B	17. C	29. B
6.B	18. C	30. D
7.D	19. D	31. A
8.B	20. C	32. B
9.B	21. D	33. C
10.D	22. A	34. A
11.D	23. D	35. D
12.A	24. B	36. D

37. A	49. C	61. C
38. C	50. A	62. A
39. A	51. A	63. B
40. C	52. A	64. D
41. C	53. A	65. A
42. B	54. A	66. A
43. B	55. A	67. B
44. C	56. B	68. D
45. C	57. B	69. A
46. B	58. C	70. A
47. D	59. A	71. D
48. D	60. C	72. A

73. A	85. D	97. A
74. D	86. B	98. C
75. C	87. D	99. C
76. B	88. A	100. D
77. A	89. D	101. A
78. C	90. A	102. D
79. A	91. A	103. C
80. B	92. A	104. A
81. D	93. A	105. C
82. A	94. D	106. B
83. D	95. A	107. B
84. B	96. C	108. C

109.A	121.A	133.A
110.C	122.B	134.A
111.D	123.A	135.A
112.A	124.A	136.C
113.C	125.D	137.A
114.B	126.B	138.A
115.C	127.A	139.C
116.A	128.D	140.A
117.D	129.D	141.D
118.D	130.B	142.A
119.B	131.A	143.D
120.A	132.A	144.B

145.C	157.A	169.B
146.A	158.D	170.D
147.B	159.D	171.A
148.A	160.D	172.C
149.A	161.D	173.D
150.C	162.B	174.A
151.D	163.D	175.A
152.C	164.D	176.A
153.D	165.A	177.D
154.A	166.C	178.A
155.C	167.D	179.D
156.D	168.B	180.B

PLEASE GIVE US YOUR FEEDBACK!

Please send us your feedback on this workbook. We would love to hear what you enjoyed most, and ways you think it could be improved!

Please Send an email to: MyBibleWorkbooks@gmail.com, or leave us a comment on one of our social media pages.

MyBibleWorkbooks@gmail.com

Projectkingdomcome

Projectkingdomcome

SCAN ME

"And I am certain that God, who began the good work within you, will continue His work until it is finally finished on the day when Christ Jesus returns. Philippians 1:6"

DRAW HERE

DRAW HERE

DRAW HERE

DRAW HERE